Trient Press

JUST

BY: ASHLEY W. PATRICK

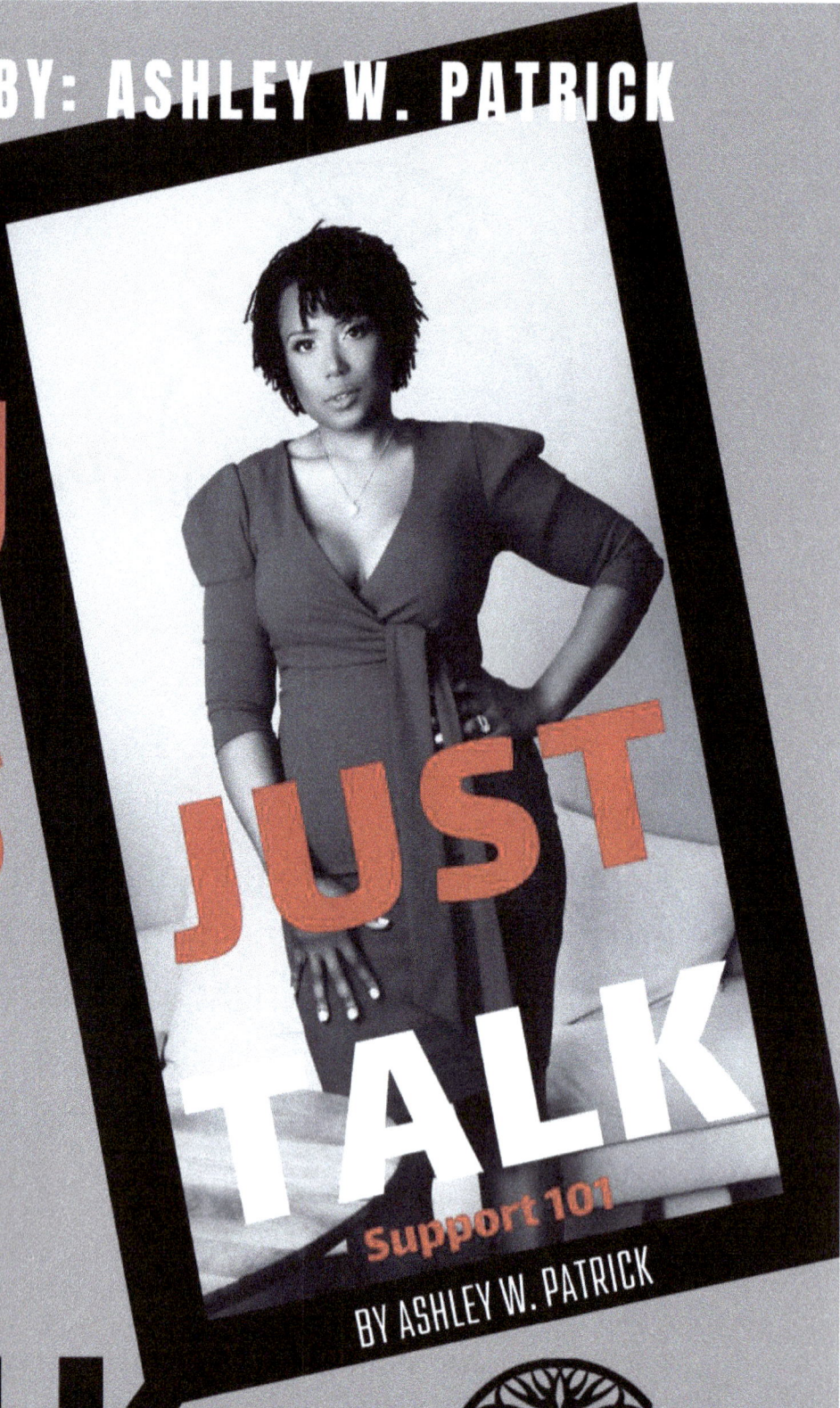

JUST

TALK

Support 101

BY ASHLEY W. PATRICK

TALK

Trient Press

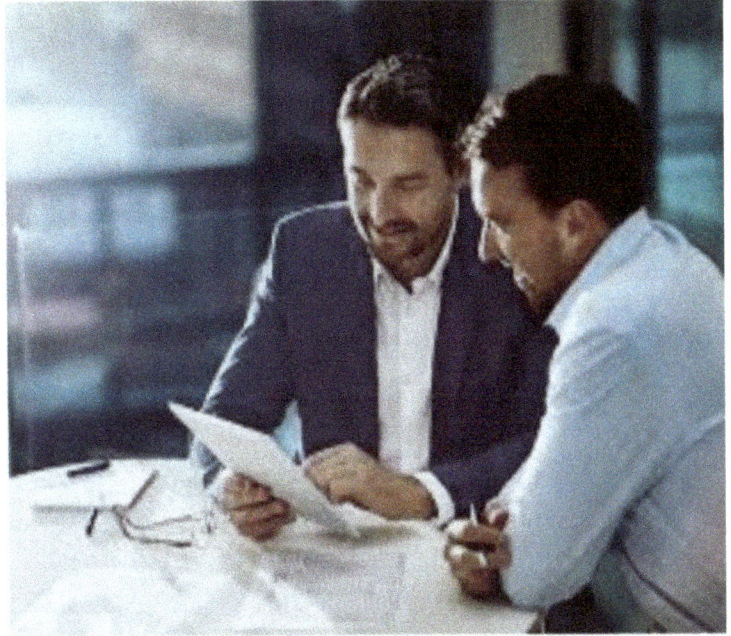

TRIENTREPRENEUR

ISSUE 12

Editor-in-Chief
Head Staff-Writer
Melisa Ruscsak

Managing Editor
Graphic Design Editor
Kristina Wenzl-Figueroa

FABLES OF THE FANTASTIC

A COLLECTION OF SHORT STORIES

DEAUNNA MARIE SMITH

Trient Press®

MARCH/ APRIL AUTHOR TIPS

Write Like a Pro: Top Ten Tips for Achieving Your Writing Goals.

- Set specific, measurable goals. Rather than simply aiming to "write more," set a specific word count or page count goal for each writing session.
- Break larger goals down into smaller, manageable tasks. Instead of trying to write a whole book at once, break it down into chapters or sections and focus on completing one at a time.
- Create a schedule and stick to it. Set aside dedicated writing time each day or week, and make it a priority to show up and write during that time.
- Eliminate distractions. Find a quiet space to write, turn off your phone and other devices, and focus solely on your writing during your scheduled writing time.
- Find an accountability partner. Share your goals with someone else who can help keep you on track and provide encouragement and support.
- Celebrate small successes. Acknowledge and celebrate each milestone you reach along the way, such as completing a chapter or reaching a word count goal.
- Stay flexible. Be open to adjusting your goals or schedule as needed to accommodate unexpected events or changes in your writing process.
- Get feedback from others. Share your work with beta readers, writing groups, or other trusted sources to get feedback and insights that can help you improve and stay motivated.
- Take breaks and recharge. Writing can be a mentally and emotionally demanding task, so make sure to take breaks and prioritize self-care to avoid burnout.
- Stay focused on your why. Remember why you started writing in the first place, and stay focused on your passion and purpose to help you stay motivated and achieve your goals.

OVERCOMING WRITER'S BLOCK: TECHNIQUES TO BOOST YOUR CREATIVITY

Unlocking Your Creative Potential: Breaking Through Writer's Block

Hey y'all! Are you a writer struggling to put pen to paper or fingers to keyboard? Well, don't you worry, because I've got some tips to help you overcome that pesky writer's block and get your creativity flowing like a wild river.

First things first, let's talk about what writer's block actually is. It's that feeling of being stuck, unable to come up with ideas, or feeling like everything you write is garbage. We've all been there, trust me.

Now, there's no one-size-fits-all solution to writer's block, but there are some techniques you can try out to help you get unstuck. Let's dive in!

Take a Break

Sometimes, the best thing you can do when you're stuck is to step away from your writing for a bit. Go for a walk, watch some TV, take a nap - whatever helps you relax and clear your mind. When you come back to your writing, you might find that your brain has had some time to process ideas and come up with something new.

NEWS PROVIDED BY: Trient Press

FREEWRITING
IF YOU'RE HAVING TROUBLE COMING UP WITH IDEAS, TRY FREEWRITING. THIS IS WHERE YOU SET A TIMER FOR 10-15 MINUTES AND JUST WRITE DOWN WHATEVER COMES TO MIND. DON'T WORRY ABOUT GRAMMAR, SPELLING, OR WHETHER OR NOT IT MAKES SENSE. THE GOAL IS TO GET YOUR BRAIN WARMED UP AND YOUR CREATIVITY FLOWING.

Change Your Environment

Sometimes, a change of scenery can do wonders for your creativity. If you're used to writing at your desk, try going to a coffee shop or park. If you're feeling really adventurous, take a weekend trip somewhere new. Exposure to new sights, sounds, and experiences can help you come up with fresh ideas.

Collaborate

Sometimes, bouncing ideas off someone else can help you break through your writer's block. Find a writing partner or join a writing group where you can share your work and get feedback. Not only will this help you generate new ideas, but it will also give you accountability to keep writing.

WRITER'S BLOCK?

Read and Research

Reading other writers' works can be a great source of inspiration. Pick up a book in your genre, or even try reading something completely different. You might find that other writers' styles and techniques spark new ideas for you. Additionally, doing research on a topic related to your writing can help you come up with new angles and ideas.

Play Games

Lastly, don't forget to have fun! There are plenty of writing games and exercises out there that can help you break out of a creative rut. Try writing a story using only 50 words, or use random words to create a poem. The point is to get your brain working in new ways and have fun while doing it.

There you have it, folks - six techniques to help you overcome writer's block and get your creativity flowing. Remember, everyone struggles with writer's block from time to time, so don't get discouraged. Just keep writing, and eventually, you'll break through. Happy writing!

Book One

Fixing The BROKEN

Without Being Broken

Turning on the light, so change can take place

FORWORD WRITTEN BY
MILLIONAIRE MOGUE AND BUSINESSMAN ANTONIO T. SMITH JR.

JEROME REDD

Trient Press®

MAKE IT STOP

END HUMAN TRAFFICKING

People are not for sale. Help us stop this
terrible happening today.

LEARN ABOUT WHAT YOU CAN DO
HTTPS://STOP-HUMANTRAFFICKING.COM

Writing Through Obstacles: Stories of Resilience and Success

Hello there, dear readers! Today, I want to share with you some incredible stories of writers who have faced obstacles, but have persevered and found success. Writing can be a tough gig, but these writers prove that with resilience and determination, anything is possible.

J.K. Rowling: The Queen of Resilience

J.K. Rowling's story is a great example of resilience in the face of rejection. After graduating from university, Rowling found herself living in poverty as a single mother, with little support and few job prospects. However, she still made time to write, often scribbling down her ideas on napkins or scraps of paper.

She spent years working on her first novel, Harry Potter and the Philosopher's Stone, but faced rejection after rejection from publishers. In fact, she was rejected by twelve publishers before finally finding a home for her manuscript at Bloomsbury Publishing. Even then, the publisher asked her to use her initials instead of her full name because they thought young boys wouldn't want to read a book written by a woman.

Despite these setbacks, Rowling never gave up. She kept writing and refining her craft, and eventually, the Harry Potter series became a global phenomenon, selling over 500 million copies worldwide and inspiring a generation of young readers.

What's particularly inspiring about Rowling's story is that she didn't achieve success overnight. It took years of hard work, determination, and countless rejections to get to where she is today. But, through it all, she never lost faith in her writing or her vision for the Harry Potter series.

Rowling's resilience has inspired countless writers around the world to keep pursuing their dreams, even in the face of rejection and setbacks. Her story is a testament to the power of perseverance and the belief in oneself, and a reminder that success is possible for anyone who is willing to work for it.

Stephen King: Journey to Success

Stephen King's journey to success is another great example of resilience and persistence in the face of rejection. Like J.K. Rowling, King faced numerous rejections before finding success as a writer.

After completing his first novel, Carrie, King submitted it to publishers, only to receive rejection after rejection. Undeterred, he continued to write, submitting manuscripts and short stories to various publications. He eventually sold some of his short stories, which helped him build a following and gain recognition as a writer.

Despite these small victories, King's path to success was still a rocky one. He faced personal and professional setbacks, including a serious car accident that left him with injuries and struggling to write. But, he never lost his passion for writing and continued to push himself to create new works.

Finally, in 1973, King's perseverance paid off when Carrie was published by Doubleday. The novel became a bestseller and launched King's career as a successful writer of horror and suspense novels. Today, King is one of the most successful and prolific writers of our time, with over 350 million copies of his books sold worldwide.

King's story is a testament to the importance of perseverance, even when facing rejection and setbacks. By continuing to write and improve his craft, King was eventually able to achieve success and become a household name in the world of literature. His story serves as an inspiration to aspiring writers everywhere, reminding us that with hard work, determination, and a love for our craft, anything is possible.

Unleashing the Power of
Marketing for
Entrepreneurial Success

Building Your Brand

Entrepreneurs often underestimate the power of branding. Your brand is how people perceive your business, and it can make or break your success. In this article, I will share some marketing tips and tricks for building your brand and creating a strong online presence.

Firstly, let's talk about the importance of having a clear brand message. Your brand message is what sets you apart from your competitors and attracts your ideal customers. Your brand message should be clear, concise, and consistent across all platforms. Make sure to articulate your value proposition and what makes your business unique.

Secondly, social media is an essential tool for building your brand. It is a free and effective way to reach a large audience and build relationships with your customers. However, you need to use it strategically. Don't just post random content, but instead create a social media strategy that aligns with your brand message and goals. Use social media to engage with your followers, showcase your products or services, and share your story.

Melisa Ruscsak
Editor-in-Chief

Trient Press Magazine

MARCH / APRIL 2023

Thirdly, consider influencer marketing. Influencer marketing involves partnering with social media influencers to promote your brand. This can be a highly effective way to reach a new audience and build trust with potential customers. However, make sure to choose influencers who align with your brand values and have a genuine connection with their followers.

> By taking action, you are one step closer to the life you always desire!

Fourthly, use video marketing to showcase your brand. Video content is highly engaging and can help you build a strong emotional connection with your audience. Consider creating product demos, behind-the-scenes footage, or customer testimonials. Use video content to tell your brand story and showcase your values.

Fifthly, use email marketing to nurture your leads and stay top of mind with your customers. Email marketing can help you build a strong relationship with your customers and drive sales. However, make sure to provide value in your emails and avoid spamming your customers with irrelevant content.

Sixthly, consider partnering with other businesses to expand your reach. Collaborating with other businesses can help you reach a new audience and build credibility. Look for businesses that share your brand values and have a similar target audience.

Seventhly, don't forget about offline marketing tactics. While online marketing is important, offline marketing can help you reach customers in your local community. Consider sponsoring local events, hosting workshops or seminars, or advertising in local media outlets.

Lastly, don't be afraid to experiment with new marketing strategies. The marketing landscape is constantly changing, and what works today may not work tomorrow. Stay up to date with the latest trends and try new tactics to see what works best for your brand.

repreneur

for Authors & Entrepreneurs

$10.99

rientrepreneur

ent Press Publication for Authors & Entrepreneurs

$10.99

ue 4 | July 2021

ATURED
er Special Agent,
Author Link

ARTICLES
ur Time Management
Tactics for Busy
ntrepreneurs

..lism Can Help
nd Strengthen
the Mind

TIPS
Must have information
for both authors and
entrepreneurs

entrepreneur

..blication for Authors & Entrepreneurs

$10.99

TRIENTREPRENEUR
MAGAZINE
WHAT'S IN YOUR TOOL BOX

PODCASTING
PROFIT SECRETS

Trient Press

Spotlight on a Successful Business
Behind the Scenes of the Austin, Texas Selfie Museum

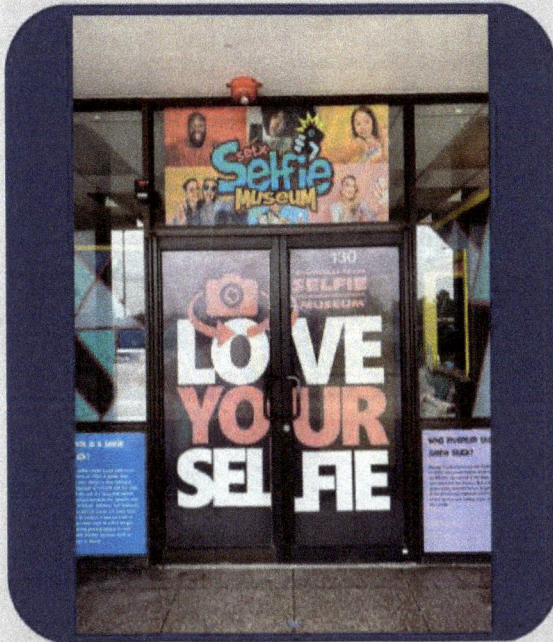

The Austin Texas Selfie Museum is a beloved destination for locals and tourists alike, known for its unique exhibits and Instagram-worthy photo opportunities. But what goes on behind the scenes of this successful business? I spoke with several employees who wished to remain anonymous to find out.

First and foremost, it's clear that the success of the Austin Texas Selfie Museum comes from the dedication and hard work of its employees. "We have a great team here," said one employee. "Everyone is passionate about making sure visitors have a memorable experience."

This dedication extends to the creation of new exhibits as well. "We spend a lot of time brainstorming ideas and putting together the exhibits," another employee shared. "It's really a team effort and we're all proud of what we've created."

But it's not all glamour and fun. The Austin Texas Selfie Museum, like any business, has faced its fair share of challenges. "There have been times when we've had to deal with difficult visitors or technical issues with the exhibits," said one employee. "But we always pull together as a team and find a solution."

Despite these challenges, the employees I spoke with expressed their gratitude for working at the Austin Texas Selfie Museum. "It's a fun environment and we get to be creative every day," one employee said. "We also have a great boss who values our input and supports us."

However, the employees also acknowledged that working in the service industry can be tough, especially during busy periods. "It can be exhausting sometimes, but it's worth it to see visitors enjoying themselves," one employee shared.

When asked about their hopes for the future of the Austin Texas Selfie Museum, the employees were optimistic. "I think we'll continue to grow and expand our reach," said one employee. "There's always room for new and exciting exhibits."

Overall, it's clear that the success of the Austin Texas Selfie Museum comes from the hard work and dedication of its employees. "We're a team here, and we all take pride in making sure visitors have a great experience," one employee said. "It's not just a job, it's a passion."

Maya Angelou: The Power of Resilience in the Face of Adversity

Maya Angelou's life and work are a testament to the power of resilience in the face of adversity. Born into poverty and segregation, Angelou faced numerous obstacles throughout her life, including racism, sexual abuse, and poverty. Despite these challenges, she never lost her passion for writing and storytelling.

Angelou's writing career began with her first memoir, I Know Why the Caged Bird Sings, which was published in 1969. The book was an instant success, earning critical acclaim and helping to establish Angelou as a major literary voice. Over the course of her career, Angelou went on to write several more memoirs, as well as poetry, essays, and other works.

Throughout her writing career, Angelou faced numerous obstacles and setbacks, including bouts of writer's block, financial struggles, and personal tragedies. But she never let these challenges stop her from pursuing her passion for writing and advocating for social justice. In fact, her experiences with adversity and discrimination only fueled her writing, inspiring her to use her voice to speak out against injustice and inequality.

Beyond her literary achievements, Angelou was also a prominent civil rights activist and a champion for women's rights. Her activism and advocacy work helped to pave the way for future generations of writers and activists, and her legacy continues to inspire people around the world today.

Angelou's story is a powerful reminder that we can overcome even the most difficult obstacles when we have a strong sense of purpose and a willingness to persevere. Despite facing unimaginable adversity, Angelou never gave up on her dreams, and her work continues to inspire and uplift readers around the world.

What can we learn from their stories?

These are just a few examples of writers who faced obstacles, but didn't let them stop their creative dreams. So, what can we learn from their stories? Here are a few key takeaways:

1. Perseverance is key. Writing can be a tough and sometimes lonely road, but if you keep at it, you will eventually find success.
2. Don't be afraid of rejection. Every writer faces rejection at some point - it's just part of the process. Use it as a learning opportunity and keep moving forward.
3. Use your experiences as fuel for your writing. Maya Angelou's life experiences informed much of her writing, and her work has had a profound impact on readers around the world.
4. Seek out support. Writing can be a solitary activity, but it doesn't have to be. Join a writing group, take a class, or attend a conference - you'll meet other writers who understand the struggles and can offer support and encouragement.

5. Believe in yourself. It's easy to doubt your abilities and question whether you're good enough, but remember that you are the only one who can tell your story. Believe in yourself and your unique voice.

Of course, these are just a few lessons we can learn from these writers' stories. But, there are countless other examples of writers who have overcome obstacles and found success. So, if you're feeling discouraged or stuck in your own writing journey, take heart - you're not alone, and there is always a way forward.

In conclusion, I hope these stories of resilience and success have inspired you to keep writing, no matter what obstacles may come your way. Remember, writing is a journey, and it's not always an easy one. But, with perseverance, determination, and a little bit of luck, anything is possible. Happy writing, dear readers!

New Releases

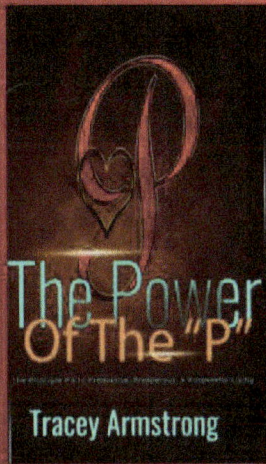

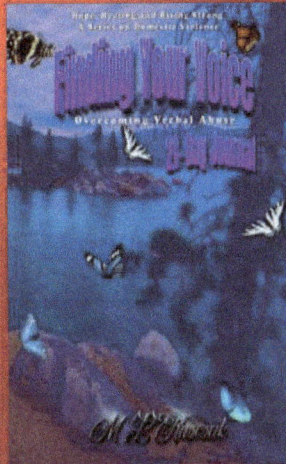

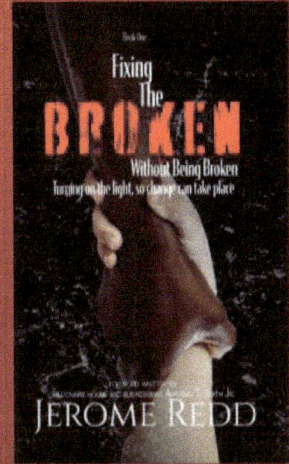

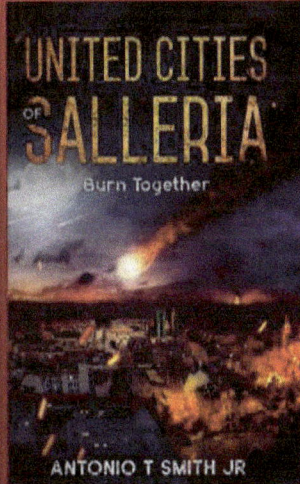

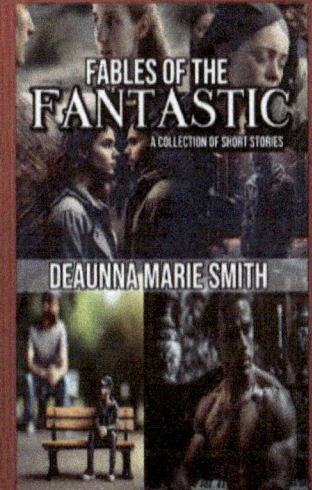

ENTREPRENEUR TIPS AND TRICKS

From Automation to Resilience

- Automate your business processes: Take advantage of automation tools to streamline your workflows, save time, and reduce errors. Consider using tools like Zapier, IFTTT, or Trello to automate repetitive tasks and improve productivity.

- Prioritize your mental health: As an entrepreneur, it's easy to get caught up in the hustle and bustle of running a business. However, it's important to prioritize your mental health and well-being. Take time each day to meditate, exercise, or do something that helps you relax and recharge.

- Build a strong personal brand: In today's digital age, building a strong personal brand is essential for entrepreneurs. Make sure your social media profiles and website are up-to-date and consistent with your brand message. Consider working with a branding expert or investing in online courses to help you develop your personal brand.

- Network strategically: Networking is key to building relationships and growing your business. However, it's important to network strategically and focus on building relationships with people who are aligned with your goals and values. Attend events and conferences where your target audience is likely to be, and be prepared to pitch your business and make meaningful connections.

- Leverage the power of video marketing: Video is a powerful tool for marketing and can help you stand out in a crowded market. Consider creating video content that showcases your products or services, shares your expertise, or provides value to your target audience.

- Outsource tasks to experts: As an entrepreneur, you may feel like you need to do everything yourself. However, outsourcing tasks to experts can help you save time and improve the quality of your work. Consider hiring a virtual assistant, social media manager, or other freelance professional to help you with tasks like content creation, bookkeeping, or customer service.

- Stay on top of industry trends: To stay competitive, it's important to stay up-to-date on industry trends and changes. Subscribe to industry publications and newsletters, attend conferences and webinars, and join industry groups on social media to stay informed.

- Focus on customer experience: Your customers are the lifeblood of your business, so it's important to prioritize their experience. Make sure your website is easy to navigate, respond promptly to customer inquiries, and seek out feedback to continually improve your products and services.

- Learn to delegate: Delegating tasks to others can be a challenge for many entrepreneurs, but it's an essential skill for growing your business. Learn to trust your team and delegate tasks that are outside of your expertise or that can be done more efficiently by someone else.

- Practice resilience: Finally, remember that entrepreneurship can be a bumpy road, with ups and downs along the way. Practice resilience and learn to bounce back from setbacks and failures. Seek out support from mentors, friends, or family members, and remember that every failure is an opportunity to learn and grow.

GOAL-SETTING FOR ENTREPRENEURS: STRATEGIES FOR SUCCESS

NEWS PROVIDED BY: TRIENT PRESS

Starting a business is an exciting and rewarding endeavor, but it can also be challenging and overwhelming. One of the keys to success as an entrepreneur is setting clear and achievable goals. In this chapter, we will explore the importance of goal-setting for entrepreneurs and provide strategies for setting and achieving your goals.

Why Set Goals?

Setting goals is essential for entrepreneurs for several reasons. First, it helps you to focus your efforts and resources on the most important tasks. When you have a clear goal in mind, you can prioritize your time and energy to achieve that goal.

Second, setting goals helps you to measure progress and track success. By setting specific, measurable goals, you can monitor your progress and adjust your strategies as needed to achieve success.

Finally, goal-setting helps you to stay motivated and committed to your vision. When you have a clear goal in mind, it can provide a sense of purpose and direction, which can help you stay motivated during challenging times.

STRATEGIES FOR SETTING AND ACHIEVING GOALS:

1. Start with your vision:
Before you can set specific goals, it's important to have a clear vision of what you want to achieve. Your vision should be a broad, long-term goal that reflects your overall mission as an entrepreneur. It should be aspirational and inspiring, and provide direction for your business.

2. Break it down:
Once you have a clear vision, break it down into smaller, specific goals. These should be goals that are achievable within a shorter timeframe, such as six months to a year. By breaking your vision down into smaller goals, you can create a roadmap for achieving your overall vision.

3. Make them SMART:
When setting your goals, it's important to make them SMART: Specific, Measurable, Achievable, Relevant, and Time-bound. This means that your goals should be clear, well-defined, and have a specific deadline for completion.

4. Write them down:
Once you have set your goals, write them down. This helps to make them more tangible and serves as a reminder of what you are working towards. You can also track your progress and celebrate your successes along the way.

5. Stay flexible:
While it's important to have a clear plan and roadmap for achieving your goals, it's also important to stay flexible. As you work towards your goals, you may encounter unexpected challenges or opportunities. Being flexible and adaptable can help you adjust your strategies and stay on track towards achieving your goals.

6. Hold yourself accountable:
Finally, hold yourself accountable for achieving your goals. Share them with others and seek feedback and support. Having someone to hold you accountable can help you stay motivated and focused on your goals.

OVERCOMING
Business Setbacks:
STORIES OF RESILIENCE AND GROWTH

Business

As an entrepreneur, setbacks are inevitable. Whether it's a failed product launch, a major client pulling out, or a global pandemic disrupting your industry, setbacks can be difficult to navigate. But the good news is that setbacks don't have to define your business. In fact, some of the most successful entrepreneurs have experienced setbacks and used them as opportunities for growth and resilience. In this article, we'll explore the stories of three entrepreneurs who overcame setbacks and emerged stronger than ever.

NEW PERSPECTIVE

First up is Sarah, the founder of a startup that was developing a new software tool for small businesses. Sarah had secured significant funding from investors and had a team of talented developers working on the product. But after months of development, Sarah realized that the product wasn't meeting the needs of her target audience. Instead of giving up, Sarah decided to pivot her business and focus on a different software tool that she had previously dismissed as a secondary product. This new tool turned out to be a hit with her target audience and helped the business grow in unexpected ways.

Next, let's talk about John, the owner of a small retail store that specialized in handmade goods. John had built up a loyal customer base over the years, but when the COVID-19 pandemic hit, he was forced to close his store temporarily.

With no online presence and limited resources, John wasn't sure how to keep his business afloat. But instead of giving up, John decided to pivot his business and start selling his products online. He quickly set up an e-commerce store and began advertising on social media. To his surprise, the online sales started pouring in, and John's business not only survived but thrived during the pandemic.

Finally, let's look at the story of Maria, the CEO of a healthcare technology company. Maria had secured a major contract with a large hospital system, which she believed would be a game-changer for her business. But when the hospital system suddenly pulled out of the contract, Maria was left reeling. Instead of dwelling on the setback, Maria used it as an opportunity to reassess her business strategy. She realized that she had become too reliant on one large client and needed to diversify her client base. She began reaching out to other hospitals and healthcare providers and was eventually able to secure new contracts that helped her business grow even stronger than before.

The stories of Sarah, John, and Maria show us that setbacks can be opportunities for growth and resilience. Instead of giving up, these entrepreneurs used setbacks as opportunities to pivot their businesses, reassess their strategies, and emerge stronger than ever. So the next time you face a setback in your business, remember that it's not the end of the road. Take a step back, reassess your strategy, and keep moving forward. Who knows, it could be the start of something great.

As you've seen from the stories of these successful entrepreneurs, setbacks and failures are simply part of the journey to success. The key is to develop a resilient mindset and to learn from your mistakes. When faced with obstacles, don't give up or lose hope. Instead, use these setbacks as an opportunity to grow and improve. Remember to stay focused on your goals, stay positive, and keep pushing forward. By adopting these strategies and learning from the experiences of others, you can overcome any setback and achieve the success you deserve. So the next time you encounter a setback, remember these stories of resilience and growth, and use them to fuel your own journey to success.

For more tips and ideas to become a successful business owner find us at www.trientpressmagazine.com.

Coming April 4
By: M.L. Ruscsak

Working For Your Dreams
THE COMPLETE
Guide to

AFFILIATE
MARKETING

M.L. Ruscsak

Trient Press

Navigating Changes in Your Industry: Tips from Successful Business Owners

As an entrepreneur, you know that change is inevitable in any industry. Whether it's advancements in technology, shifts in consumer behavior, or unexpected market disruptions, you must be prepared to adapt and evolve to stay competitive. Fortunately, you're not alone in this challenge. Many successful business owners have faced and overcome similar obstacles. In this article, we'll explore their tips and strategies for navigating changes in your industry.

1. Stay on Top of Industry Trends

The first step in successfully navigating industry changes is staying informed. Regularly researching and monitoring trends within your industry can help you anticipate potential challenges and identify opportunities for growth. You can do this by attending conferences, subscribing to industry publications, and following relevant thought leaders on social media.

Take the example of Emily Weiss, founder of beauty brand Glossier. Weiss recognized early on that traditional beauty brands were not resonating with younger consumers. She used her industry knowledge to create a brand that was more authentic and relatable, meeting the demands of this growing market.

2. Be Willing to Take Risks

Navigating industry changes often requires taking risks. This may mean investing in new technology, entering into partnerships, or pivoting your business model altogether. It can be tempting to stick to what you know, but successful entrepreneurs understand the importance of being willing to take calculated risks.

Consider the story of Jeff Bezos, founder of Amazon. When he first launched the company, it was an online bookstore. However, Bezos recognized the potential for growth in the e-commerce market and took a risk by expanding Amazon's offerings to include a wide range of products. This move paid off, and Amazon is now one of the most successful and influential companies in the world.

3. Stay Agile and Flexible

In a rapidly changing industry, it's crucial to remain agile and flexible. This means being open to change and willing to pivot your strategy as needed. You may need to adjust your business model, marketing approach, or product offerings to stay relevant and meet the evolving needs of your customers.

Take the example of Starbucks. The coffee giant has always been known for its in-store experience, but when the COVID-19 pandemic hit, they quickly pivoted to offer more online ordering and delivery options. This flexibility allowed them to continue serving customers during a challenging time and may have even opened up new revenue streams for the company.

4. Build Strong Relationships

Building strong relationships with customers, suppliers, and partners can help you navigate industry changes more effectively. Your customers are your best source of feedback and can help you understand what they need and want from your business. Meanwhile, partnerships with other businesses can help you access new markets or technologies that can drive growth.

Take the example of Elon Musk, CEO of Tesla. Musk has built strong relationships with suppliers and partners, allowing him to secure the resources he needs to innovate and develop cutting-edge technologies. Additionally, his customer-centric approach has helped him build a dedicated and loyal following for his brand.

Take the example of Patagonia, an outdoor clothing brand known for its commitment to sustainability. The company invests heavily in employee training and development, ensuring that its team members are knowledgeable about sustainable practices and can help drive the company's mission forward.

6. Staying True to Your Values
Entrepreneurs can successfully navigate industry changes and come out on top.

5. Invest in Your Employees
Investing in your employees can help your business navigate industry changes more effectively. Your team members are your most valuable asset, and providing them with ongoing training and development opportunities can help them stay up-to-date on the latest industry trends and best practices. Additionally, fostering a culture of innovation and creativity can encourage your team to come up with new ideas and solutions that can help your business stay ahead of the curve.

- One of the most important factors in successfully navigating industry changes is staying informed about trends and developments in your industry. This means not only keeping up with the latest news and updates, but also actively seeking out new information and perspectives. Attend industry conferences, join industry associations, and network with other entrepreneurs and business leaders in your field. By staying plugged in to your industry, you'll be better equipped to anticipate changes and adapt your strategy accordingly.

- Another key to success in the face of industry changes is taking calculated risks. This doesn't mean making reckless decisions, but rather taking strategic risks that have the potential to pay off in the long run. Be willing to try new things, experiment with new technologies or business models, and pursue opportunities that others may overlook. Of course, it's important to balance risk-taking with caution and good judgment, but by embracing a mindset of calculated risk-taking, you'll be better positioned to thrive in a changing industry.

- Remaining agile and flexible is also crucial when navigating industry changes. As we've seen with Disney, adaptability is key to staying relevant and successful over the long term. This means being open to new ideas, willing to pivot your strategy when needed, and staying nimble in the face of shifting market dynamics. Don't be afraid to make changes to your business model, product offerings, or marketing strategy if it means staying ahead of the curve.

- Building strong relationships with customers, employees, partners, and other stakeholders is another essential ingredient in successfully navigating industry changes. By fostering trust, loyalty, and engagement among your stakeholders, you'll be better able to weather storms and overcome challenges. This means investing in customer service, fostering a positive company culture, and building strong partnerships with other businesses and organizations in your industry.

- Finally, it's important to stay true to your values and mission when navigating industry changes. This means keeping your company's core values and mission front and center, even as you adapt to new challenges and opportunities. By staying true to your roots, you'll be able to maintain the trust and loyalty of your customers, employees, and stakeholders, even as you evolve and grow.

- In conclusion, navigating industry changes is a challenge that every entrepreneur will face at some point. By staying informed, taking calculated risks, remaining agile and flexible, building strong relationships, and staying true to their values, entrepreneurs can successfully navigate industry changes and come out on top. Remember that industry changes are an opportunity to innovate, experiment, and grow, and with the right mindset and approach, you can turn even the biggest challenges into new opportunities for success.

Antonio T. Smith Jr:
Author, Keynote Speaker, and Visionary

M.L. Ruscsak

Antonio T. Smith Jr is a motivational speaker, author, and entrepreneur who has made a name for himself as a passionate advocate for personal development and success. His life's work is centered around helping people overcome their fears, limiting beliefs, and negative self-talk so that they can live their best lives. Smith's journey began in humble beginnings, growing up in a small town in Texas where he experienced poverty, abuse, and adversity. Despite these challenges, Smith found a way to rise above his circumstances and create a life that he could be proud of. He began his career as a car salesman, but quickly realized that his true passion was in helping people achieve their dreams. Over the years, Smith has honed his skills as a speaker and mentor, delivering powerful talks and coaching sessions that inspire people to take action and achieve their goals. He has worked with thousands of clients, from CEOs and executives to everyday people looking to improve their lives. His message is simple but powerful: "Your past does not determine your future. You have the power to create the life you want."

Antonio T. Smith Jr, known for his non-fiction works on personal development and success, has now made a name for himself as a sought-after fictional author with The United Cities of Salleria, Burn Together. The novel's fast-paced storyline is full of action, suspense, and danger at every turn. Ashton is a member of a secretive society of assassins and has risen to become one of the greatest Special Forces soldiers of all time.

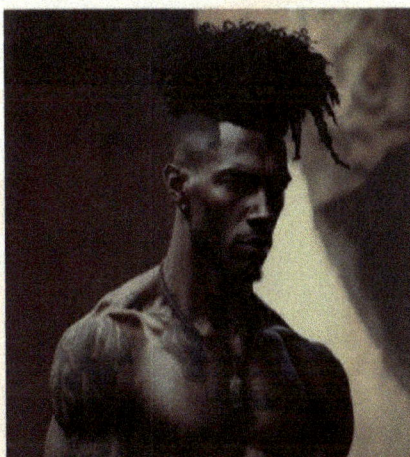

Meet Ashton, also known as "The Ghost" - a skilled Special Forces soldier and assassin who is the protagonist of The United Cities of Salleria, Burn Together. In this gripping novel, readers are taken on a thrilling journey as Ashton faces his toughest mission yet - battling an enemy army and a group of vengeful serial killers.

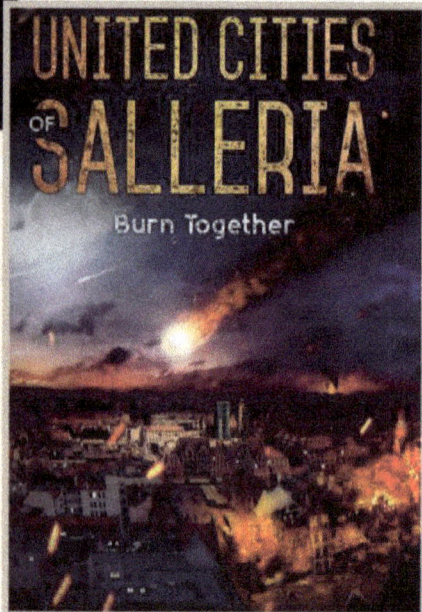

Ashton's latest mission for the United Cities of Salleria sparks World War III when the North Kangavarian military launches a series of EMP attacks and invades the United Cities, leading to the deaths of millions of innocent civilians. Meanwhile, a convicted serial killer who harbors a grudge against Ashton escapes from a Supermax Prison and sets out to hunt down and murder everyone responsible for his incarceration. Ashton becomes his primary target, and the assassin must use all his skills and resources to stay alive while he saves the world from destruction.

The United Cities of Salleria, Burn Together is a heart-pumping read that is sure to keep readers on the edge of their seats until the very last page. It is a must-read for anyone who loves action-packed thrillers, and Antonio T. Smith Jr's transition from non-fiction to fiction has been a successful one, showcasing his versatility as an author. Join Ashton on his dangerous mission, navigating through assassins, war, and survival.

In addition to his work as an author, Smith is also a sought-after keynote speaker, delivering talks on a wide range of topics including personal development, entrepreneurship, and leadership. He has spoken at conferences, seminars, and events across the country, inspiring audiences with his powerful message and engaging delivery.

One of the things that sets Smith apart from other speakers and authors is his focus on community building and collaboration. He understands that success is not just about individual achievement, but about working together to create a better world for everyone. This is evident in his work with The ATS Jr Companies, a group of companies that he has founded with the goal of creating opportunities for people to achieve success in all areas of their lives.

Whether through his books, speeches, or entrepreneurial ventures, Antonio T. Smith Jr is a visionary leader who is changing the world one person at a time. His commitment to personal development, community building, and positive change is an inspiration to all who meet him.

Coming Soon

BY:
ANTONIO T. SMITH JR.

KOFI SAI
AND THE ANANSI GUARDIANS
ANTONIO T SMITH JR

The Power of Networking:

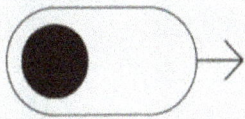

Antonio T. Smith Jr.'s Strategies for Building a Strong Professional Network

Building a strong professional network is one of the most valuable assets any entrepreneur can have. Connections can open doors to new opportunities, provide insights and knowledge, and offer support during difficult times. One entrepreneur who knows the power of networking is Antonio T. Smith Jr. Here, we explore his strategies for building a strong professional network.

- Attend Events: One of the best ways to network is by attending events that attract like-minded individuals. Smith suggests that entrepreneurs attend events that align with their industry or interests, such as conferences, trade shows, and seminars. By attending these events, entrepreneurs can meet people in their industry, exchange ideas, and build relationships.

- Use Social Media: Social media platforms are a great way to connect with people in your industry and build relationships. Smith recommends entrepreneurs use LinkedIn to connect with professionals in their field, share their work, and engage in conversations. He also suggests using Twitter to participate in industry chats and share relevant content.

- Focus on Quality: When it comes to networking, Smith believes that quality is more important than quantity. He advises entrepreneurs to focus on building meaningful relationships with a few key people rather than collecting a large number of contacts. By focusing on quality, entrepreneurs can build relationships that are built on trust, respect, and shared interests.

- Give Value: Smith stresses the importance of giving value to others when building relationships. This can include sharing knowledge, providing resources, and making introductions. By giving value, entrepreneurs can establish themselves as thought leaders in their industry and build a reputation as someone who is willing to help others.

- Follow Up: Following up is key to maintaining relationships and keeping the lines of communication open. Smith suggests sending personalized messages to people after meeting them at events or connecting with them on social media. This can help to solidify the relationship and demonstrate your interest in building a connection.

In conclusion, building a strong professional network is critical for any entrepreneur looking to succeed in their industry. Antonio T. Smith Jr.'s strategies, including attending events, using social media, focusing on quality, giving value, and following up, can help entrepreneurs build meaningful relationships that can lead to new opportunities and growth. By putting these strategies into practice, entrepreneurs can develop a strong network that can support them throughout their career.

Traveling with Trient

EXPLORING NEW HORIZONS:
TIPS FOR SAFE & AFFORDABLE TRAVEL IN 2023

Are you ready to explore new horizons in 2023? After a long period of isolation and uncertainty, it's time to start planning your next adventure. But with COVID-19 still lingering in many parts of the world, safety and affordability should be top priorities when it comes to travel planning. Here are some tips for safe and affordable travel in 2023.

DO YOUR RESEARCH

Before you book your next trip, make sure to do your research. Check the COVID-19 entry requirements for your destination, as they can change frequently. Look for destinations that have lower COVID-19 case rates and are taking safety precautions seriously. You can also check for deals and promotions on travel booking websites to save money on flights, accommodations, and activities.

BE FLEXIBLE

Flexibility is key when it comes to safe and affordable travel in 2023. Consider traveling during off-peak seasons, as prices tend to be lower and crowds are smaller. Be open to alternative destinations if your first choice is not safe or affordable at the moment. And if plans change due to unforeseen circumstances, make sure you have travel insurance that covers cancellations and medical emergencies.

STAY SAFE

Even if you are fully vaccinated, it's important to continue practicing safety precautions when traveling. Wear a mask in public spaces and on public transportation, wash your hands frequently, and practice social distancing when possible. Avoid crowded areas and events, and consider outdoor activities instead. If you're traveling internationally, make sure to register with the U.S. embassy in your destination country in case of emergencies.

SAVE MONEY ON ACCOMMODATIONS

Accommodations can be one of the biggest expenses when traveling, but there are ways to save money. Look for deals on travel booking websites, and consider staying in vacation rentals or hostels instead of hotels. You can also try house-sitting or house-swapping for free accommodations. If you're traveling with a group, consider renting a house or apartment instead of separate hotel rooms.

EXPLORE THE OUTDOORS

One of the best ways to stay safe and save money while traveling is to explore the outdoors. National parks, hiking trails, and beaches are great options for outdoor adventures. Pack a picnic lunch and enjoy the scenery, or camp overnight for a more immersive experience. Just make sure to follow safety guidelines and respect the environment.

SUPPORT LOCAL BUSINESSES

Traveling in 2023 is a great opportunity to support local businesses that may have struggled during the pandemic. Eat at local restaurants, shop at local markets, and book tours with local operators. You'll not only be supporting the local economy, but also getting a more authentic experience.

BE MINDFUL OF YOUR IMPACT

Traveling can have a big impact on the environment and local communities. Be mindful of your actions and try to minimize your impact. Don't leave trash behind, respect local customs and traditions, and be considerate of the local wildlife. You can also consider offsetting your carbon footprint by supporting carbon reduction projects.

In conclusion, traveling in 2023 can be safe and affordable if you do your research, stay flexible, and prioritize safety. By exploring the outdoors, supporting local businesses, and being mindful of your impact, you can have a memorable and responsible travel experience.

Pre-Order now!

ANTONIO T. SMITH JR.

Pre-Order now

EXPLORING NEW HORIZONS:
TIPS FOR FINDING *Inspiration* IN TRAVEL

Inspiration

to be best in...
point of view.
mind, feelings
creative act or
stimulation or

Successful Authors and Entrepreneurs:
How Travel Inspired Their Stories

By: M.L. Ruscsak

Travel is not just a leisure activity, it can also be a source of inspiration for many successful authors and entrepreneurs. From Hemingway to Branson, many accomplished individuals have found their creative spark and business ideas while exploring new horizons. In this article, we will dive into the stories of some of these successful individuals and explore how they have found inspiration through travel.

Ernest Hemingway is one of the most iconic American writers of the 20th century, and his adventurous lifestyle and travels are well-documented. Hemingway spent a significant amount of time in Spain, France, and Cuba, and his experiences in these countries greatly influenced his writing. In his novel "The Sun Also Rises," he wrote about his love for Spain and the bullfighting culture. Hemingway also spent time in Paris during the 1920s, where he was part of the "Lost Generation" of writers and artists who found inspiration in the city's vibrant culture. For Hemingway, travel was not only a way to experience new cultures but also a way to expand his creative horizons.

> *"Never go on trips with anyone you do not love."*
> *- Ernest Hemingway*

Similarly, entrepreneur Richard Branson, the founder of Virgin Group, has found inspiration through travel. Branson has traveled extensively throughout his life, and he believes that experiencing different cultures and meeting new people is crucial to his success. In a blog post, Branson stated, "Travel has always been one of my biggest inspirations. Seeing the world and all its different cultures, meeting new people and trying new things – that's what life is all about." Branson has used his travel experiences to inform his business decisions and create innovative products and services that appeal to a global market.

CASE STUDY: A COMPANY'S JOURNEY FROM FAILURE TO SUCCESS

The Walt Disney Story

In this article, we will explore the story of how Walt Disney's company went from near failure to becoming an iconic brand and a cultural touchstone.

We will start by delving into the early days of Walt Disney's career and the founding of the Disney Brothers Studio in the 1920s. Despite the success of the "Alice Comedies," which combined live-action with animation, the studio struggled financially in its early years. We will explore the factors that contributed to this, such as mismanagement and the loss of key talent.

When most people think of Walt Disney, they think of the iconic theme parks, beloved characters like Mickey Mouse and Donald Duck, and classic animated films like Snow White and the Seven Dwarfs. But before he became a household name, Walt Disney was just a struggling artist with big dreams.

Born in 1901 in Chicago, Illinois, Walt showed an early interest in art and drawing. He began taking classes at the Art Institute of Chicago when he was just 14 years old, but he dropped out of high school at age 16 to join the army. After his service ended, he moved to Kansas City, Missouri, where he got a job as a commercial artist.

In 1920, Walt and his brother Roy moved to Hollywood, California, where they founded the Disney Brothers Studio. The early days of the studio were difficult, with Walt and Roy working long hours in a small garage to produce short animated films. The brothers struggled to make ends meet, and at one point they were so broke that they had to eat dog food to survive.

But Walt was determined to succeed. He had a vision for a new kind of animated film, one that would combine the artistry of hand-drawn animation with the emotional depth of live-action movies. In 1928, that vision became a reality with the release of Steamboat Willie, the first cartoon to feature synchronized sound. The film starred Mickey Mouse, a character that Walt had created out of desperation after losing the rights to his earlier character, Oswald the Lucky Rabbit.

Steamboat Willie was a massive hit, and Mickey Mouse became an overnight sensation. The Disney Brothers Studio quickly expanded, producing more animated shorts featuring Mickey and other characters like Donald Duck and Goofy. Walt's attention to detail and dedication to quality made the Disney brand synonymous with excellence, and his innovations in animation technology set the standard for the industry.

Over the next few years, the Disney Brothers Studio continued to grow, producing longer animated features like Snow White and the Seven Dwarfs, Pinocchio, and Fantasia. These films were groundbreaking in their use of color, music, and storytelling, and they helped cement Disney's place as a major force in the entertainment industry.

But Walt's ambitions didn't stop there. In the 1950s, he turned his attention to television, creating the Disney anthology series, which featured a mix of cartoons, live-action dramas, and educational segments. He also began developing plans for a theme park that would bring his beloved characters to life.

Despite some setbacks and challenges, Walt's dream of a theme park became a reality in 1955 with the opening of Disneyland in Anaheim, California. The park was an instant success, drawing crowds from around the world and inspiring a new era of theme parks and family entertainment.

Walt Disney's career was marked by innovation, creativity, and an unwavering commitment to his vision. He transformed the world of animation and entertainment, creating a legacy that continues to inspire new generations of artists and dreamers.

Today, the Disney brand is stronger than ever, with theme parks around the world, a vast array of beloved characters, and a string of blockbuster movies that continue to captivate audiences of all ages. And it all started with a young artist with big dreams and a determination to make them a reality.

Next, we will discuss how the studio's fortunes turned around with the creation of Mickey Mouse in 1928. We will examine the impact that the character had on the company's success, as well as the innovations that Disney brought to the animation industry, such as the introduction of synchronized sound and Technicolor.

In the 1920s, Walt Disney and his brother Roy founded the Disney Brothers Studio in California. Initially, they produced a series of short films called the "Alice Comedies," which combined live-action with animation. However, the studio struggled to make a profit and faced bankruptcy multiple times.

The turning point for the studio came in 1928, with the creation of Mickey Mouse. The character was an instant hit, and the studio quickly produced a series of successful shorts featuring Mickey and other characters such as Donald Duck and Goofy.

One of the reasons for Mickey's success was the innovative use of synchronized sound. The 1928 short film "Steamboat Willie" was

the first cartoon with synchronized sound and helped to popularize the new technology in the animation industry. Disney continued to innovate with the introduction of Technicolor, which added color to their films and made them even more visually stunning.

The success of Mickey Mouse and the studio's innovations helped to cement Disney's place as a leader in the animation industry. The studio continued to produce successful shorts throughout the 1930s, and in 1937, they released their first full-length animated feature, "Snow White and the Seven Dwarfs." The film was a massive success, and it paved the way for future Disney classics such as "Cinderella" and "The Little Mermaid."

Beyond the animation industry, Disney's impact extended to other areas such as theme parks and merchandise. Disneyland, which opened in 1955, became an instant sensation and helped to popularize the concept of amusement parks. Today, Disney operates multiple theme parks around the world and is one of the largest media and entertainment companies in the world.

In conclusion, the creation of Mickey Mouse was a turning point for the Disney Brothers Studio and the animation industry as a whole. The success of the character, along with the studio's innovations in sound and color, helped to establish Disney as a leader in the industry and paved the way for future successes. Disney's impact extends beyond animation and entertainment, and the company continues to be a cultural icon today.

Walt Disney's impact on branding and marketing is just as important to the company's success as his innovations in animation.

Walt Disney's career was marked by innovation, creativity, and an unwavering commitment to his vision. He transformed the world of animation and entertainment, creating a legacy that continues to inspire new generations of artists and dreamers.

Today, the Disney brand is stronger than ever, with theme parks around the world, a vast array of beloved characters, and a string of blockbuster movies that continue to captivate audiences of all ages. And it all started with a young artist with big dreams and a determination to make them a reality.

Disney's focus on branding didn't stop with the theme park. He also established partnerships with other companies, such as the television program The Mickey Mouse Club. The show helped to solidify the company's brand and reach a wider audience. The company's characters and stories were everywhere, from lunchboxes to clothing to toys, and they all reinforced the Disney brand.

Another significant turning point for the company was Walt Disney's decision to create Walt Disney World in Florida. This massive undertaking not only gave the company a new location to expand its offerings but also served as a way to bring in revenue through tourism. Walt Disney World opened in 1971 and was an immediate success. The park featured new and innovative attractions such as the Haunted Mansion and Pirates of the Caribbean, as well as beloved classics like It's a Small World and Space Mountain.

The success of Walt Disney World helped to further cement Disney's position as a leader in the entertainment industry. Disney continued to expand its offerings with new theme parks, resorts, and attractions around the world. The company also continued to innovate in animation, with new films and techniques such as computer-generated animation.

Today, the Disney brand is known and beloved around the world. It has become a symbol of family-friendly entertainment and storytelling. The company's success can be attributed to the vision and creativity of Walt Disney, who recognized the power of branding and creating a cohesive image for his company.

Walt Disney's journey from struggling artist to media mogul is one of the most inspiring stories in American business history.

His vision, tenacity, and creativity led him to create a company that has become an iconic symbol of entertainment and imagination around the world.

Disney's success is a testament to the power of entrepreneurship and the importance of pursuing your creative vision, even when faced with skepticism and doubt. His willingness to take risks, experiment with new technologies, and think outside the box helped him to create a brand that has endured for nearly a century.

Aspiring entrepreneurs can learn a great deal from Disney's example. By focusing on quality, creating a strong brand identity, and always being willing to innovate and take risks, business leaders can follow in Disney's footsteps and achieve their own dreams of success.

In conclusion, Walt Disney's story is a reminder of the power of perseverance, creativity, and vision in achieving success. His legacy continues to inspire and entertain millions of people around the world, and his impact on the entertainment industry and American culture will be felt for generations to come.

Another successful entrepreneur who has found inspiration through travel is Airbnb co-founder Joe Gebbia. Gebbia and his co-founders launched Airbnb in 2008, and the company has since revolutionized the travel industry by allowing people to rent out their homes and apartments to travelers. Gebbia has stated that his travels have played a significant role in the development of Airbnb. He believes that travel allows people to connect with others on a deeper level and that this connection is crucial to the success of the company. Gebbia has also used his travel experiences to inform the design of Airbnb's spaces, ensuring that they are welcoming and comfortable for all guests.

In addition to Hemingway, Branson, and Gebbia, many other successful authors and entrepreneurs have found inspiration through travel. J.K. Rowling, the author of the Harry Potter series, found inspiration for the Hogwarts School of Witchcraft and Wizardry while traveling on a train. Steve Jobs, the late co-founder of Apple, found inspiration for the company's design ethos during a trip to Japan. These examples show that travel can be a powerful tool for finding inspiration and creating innovative ideas.

But what can we learn from these successful individuals? How can we use travel to find inspiration in our own lives and careers? Here are some tips:

> *"Business opportunities are like buses, there's always another one coming." - Richard Branson*

EMBRACE THE UNKNOWN
One of the most exciting things about travel is the opportunity to experience something new and different. Embrace the unknown and be open to trying new things. Whether it's trying a new food or exploring a new city, stepping outside of your comfort zone can lead to unexpected inspiration.

IMMERSE YOURSELF IN THE CULTURE
To truly experience a new place, you need to immerse yourself in the culture. Attend local festivals and events, learn about the history and traditions of the area, and talk to locals to gain a deeper understanding of the culture. This can provide valuable insights that can inform your work and creative endeavors.

TAKE TIME TO REFLECT
While it's important to be active and engaged during your travels, it's also important to take time to reflect. Whether it's through journaling or simply taking a moment

EXPLORING THE BEST OF HOUSTON WITH YOUR FAMILY: A SPRING GUIDE TO RODEOS, PARKS, MUSEUMS, AND MORE!

If you're planning a family trip to Houston, Texas, in the spring, you're in luck! The city has plenty to offer for travelers of all ages, from outdoor activities to indoor attractions. In this article, we'll explore some of the best things to do with your family in Houston, including visiting the Houston Livestock Show and Rodeo, exploring Hermann Park, visiting the Space Center Houston, and checking out the Museum District.

HOUSTON LIVESTOCK SHOW AND RODEO

One of the biggest events in Houston during the spring is the Houston Livestock Show and Rodeo. This annual event, usually held in March, is one of the largest rodeos in the world, attracting over 2.5 million visitors each year. The event features live music from top performers, carnival rides, and livestock exhibitions. It's a great way to experience the unique culture of Texas and see some of the best rodeo performers in the world.

HERMANN PARK

For a more relaxed day out with the family, head to Hermann Park. This park is a great spot to enjoy the spring weather with its gardens, walking trails, and pedal boats. The park features several attractions, including the Houston Zoo, the Miller Outdoor Theatre, and the Japanese Garden. The Houston Zoo is home to over 6,000 animals and offers a fun and educational experience for visitors of all ages. The Miller Outdoor Theatre hosts free performances throughout the year, including music, dance, and theater. The Japanese Garden is a peaceful oasis in the heart of the park, with a koi pond, waterfall, and traditional Japanese landscaping.

SPACE CENTER HOUSTON

If your family is interested in space exploration, then a visit to Space Center Houston is a must. This attraction is the official visitor center for NASA's Johnson Space Center and offers a wide range of exhibits and interactive displays that showcase the history of space exploration and the work being done at the center today. Visitors can take a tram tour of the center, visit the astronaut gallery, and even touch a moon rock.

DISCOVERY GREEN

Another fun outdoor destination in Houston is Discovery Green. This park in downtown Houston hosts numerous events and festivals during the spring, including outdoor movie screenings, live music performances, and food truck festivals. There are also several play areas for kids, including a splash pad and a playground.

THE MUSEUM DISTRICT

Finally, no trip to Houston would be complete without a visit to the Museum District. This neighborhood is home to over 19 museums and cultural institutions, including the Museum of Fine Arts, the Houston Museum of Natural Science, and the Children's Museum of Houston. The Museum of Fine Arts features over 70,000 works of art, from ancient to modern, while the Houston Museum of Natural Science has exhibits on dinosaurs, gems and minerals, and space exploration. The Children's Museum of Houston offers interactive exhibits and educational programs designed specifically for children.

In conclusion, Houston, Texas, is a great destination for families looking for fun and educational activities in the springtime. From the Houston Livestock Show and Rodeo to the Museum District, there is something for everyone in this vibrant and exciting city.

THE DEREK HOTEL: A CHIC AND COMFORTABLE STAY IN THE HEART OF HOUSTON

If you're planning a trip to Houston, you'll want to check out The Derek Hotel. This chic and comfortable hotel is located in the heart of the Galleria area, making it the perfect place to stay for those who want to be close to shopping, dining, and other entertainment options.

As soon as you enter The Derek Hotel, you'll notice the attention to detail and modern décor. The lobby features comfortable seating areas, contemporary art, and a fireplace that creates a warm and welcoming atmosphere.

The hotel has 312 rooms and suites, all of which are spacious and tastefully decorated. The rooms feature plush bedding, flat-screen TVs, and complimentary Wi-Fi, making it easy for you to relax and stay connected during your stay.

The hotel also has several amenities that will make your stay even more enjoyable. There is a fitness center for those who want to stay active, as well as a rooftop pool and terrace for those who want to soak up the sun. Additionally, the hotel has a business center and meeting rooms for those who need to get work done during their stay.

One of the best things about The Derek Hotel is its in-house restaurant, Revolve Kitchen + Bar. This restaurant offers a modern take on classic American cuisine, using fresh and locally sourced ingredients to create delicious dishes. The restaurant is open for breakfast, lunch, and dinner, so you can enjoy a meal at any time of day.

For breakfast, you can choose from a variety of options, including buttermilk pancakes, avocado toast, and eggs benedict. The lunch menu features a selection of salads, sandwiches, and entrees, such as the grilled salmon or chicken fried steak. The dinner menu is even more impressive, with options like the bone-in ribeye, pan-seared scallops, and roasted chicken.

The restaurant also has a bar that serves craft cocktails, beer, and wine. The bartenders are skilled and knowledgeable, and can make a drink to suit any taste. If you're not sure what to order, ask for a recommendation based on your preferences.

The restaurant has a modern and comfortable atmosphere, with both indoor and outdoor seating options. The outdoor patio is especially popular, with its string lights and cozy seating areas. It's the perfect spot to enjoy a meal with friends or family. In addition to the restaurant, The Derek Hotel also has a coffee bar that serves Starbucks coffee and pastries. This is a great place to stop and grab a quick breakfast or snack on the go.

Overall, The Derek Hotel and Revolve Kitchen + Bar are a great choice for anyone visiting Houston. The hotel's prime location, modern décor, and comfortable rooms make it a popular choice, and the restaurant's delicious food and drinks are the icing on the cake. Whether you're traveling for business or pleasure, The Derek Hotel is sure to make your stay in Houston a memorable one.

In conclusion, The Derek Hotel is a fantastic option for those looking for a chic and comfortable stay in Houston. The hotel's modern décor, spacious rooms, and great amenities make it a popular choice, and the in-house restaurant, Revolve Kitchen + Bar, is sure to impress with its delicious food and drinks. Whether you're visiting Houston for business or pleasure, The Derek Hotel should be at the top of your list.

Spring Pecan Pie

INGREDIENTS

8 SERVINGS

- 1 9-INCH UNBAKED PIE CRUST
- 1 CUP LIGHT CORN SYRUP
- 1 CUP PACKED LIGHT BROWN SUGAR
- 3 EGGS
- 1/3 CUP UNSALTED BUTTER, MELTED
- 1 TEASPOON VANILLA EXTRACT
- 1/2 TEASPOON SALT
- 1 1/2 CUPS PECAN HALVES

DIRECTIONS

- Preheat the oven to 350°F.
- In a large bowl, whisk together the corn syrup, brown sugar, eggs, melted butter, vanilla extract, and salt until well combined.
- Stir in the pecan halves.
- Pour the mixture into the unbaked pie crust.
- Bake for 45 to 50 minutes, or until the filling is set and the crust is golden brown.
- Allow the pie to cool completely before slicing and serving.

Nutritional information (per serving):
Calories: 540
Fat: 29g
Saturated Fat: 9g
Cholesterol: 104mg
Sodium: 255mg
Carbohydrates: 70g
Fiber: 2g
Sugars: 56g
Protein: 5g

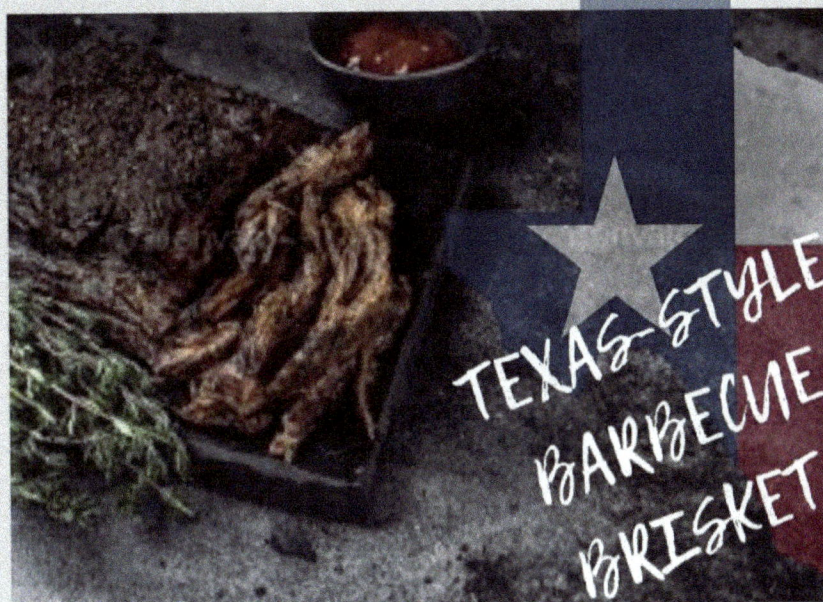

TEXAS-STYLE BARBECUE BRISKET:

Ingredients

- 1 (6-8 pound) brisket, trimmed
- 2 tablespoons paprika
- 2 tablespoons chili powder
- 2 tablespoons brown sugar
- 1 tablespoon salt
- 1 tablespoon black pepper
- 1 tablespoon garlic powder
- 1 tablespoon onion powder
- 1 tablespoon cumin
- 1 tablespoon mustard powder
- 1/2 teaspoon cayenne pepper
- 1 cup beef broth
- 1 cup barbecue sauce
- Wood chips (preferably oak or hickory)

Directions

- Preheat your smoker to 225°F.
- In a small bowl, combine the paprika, chili powder, brown sugar, salt, black pepper, garlic powder, onion powder, cumin, mustard powder, and cayenne pepper. Mix well to make a dry rub.
- Rub the brisket all over with the dry rub, making sure to coat it evenly.
- Place the brisket on the smoker, fat side up. Add wood chips to the smoker box or wrap them in foil and poke a few holes to let smoke escape.
- Smoke the brisket for 10-12 hours, or until it reaches an internal temperature of 195°F.
- Once the brisket is cooked, remove it from the smoker and wrap it tightly in foil. Let it rest for at least 30 minutes before slicing.
- While the brisket is resting, make the barbecue sauce. In a small saucepan, heat the beef broth and barbecue sauce over low heat until heated through.
- Slice the brisket against the grain into 1/4-inch slices. Serve with the barbecue sauce and your favorite sides.

Nutrition Facts

Serving size: 4 ounces of brisket Calories: 284 Fat: 12g Carbohydrates: 3g Protein: 38g.